Multicultural Clip Art

From Around the World

Susan Schneck

SCHOLASTIC
PROFESSIONAL BOOKS

NEW YORK • TORONTO • LONDON • AUCKLAND • SYDNEY

<u>Dedication</u>
To the spark of creativity in all of us!

Special thanks to
Barbara Holdridge
whose designs from the Stemmer House
International Design Library were used
in conjunction with our own development of this book.
Resource list and bibliography on pages 17 and 18 give credits.

Book design and illustrations by Susan Schneck
Cover design by Jo-Ann Rosiello
Images noted on pages 17 and 18 compiled from Stemmer House artists:
Barbara Holdridge, Caren Caraway, Anthony Chan, Pradumma and Roslba Tana,
Bev Ulsrud Van Berkom, Ramona Jablonski, and Anita Bernarde.

ISBN # 0-590-48177-0
Printed in the U.S.A.
10 9 8 7 6 5 4 3   6 7 8/9

Table of Contents

A World of Art at Your Scissor Tips

The purpose of this book is to give you a world-wide collection of ancient and current decorative art that will help you make authentic classroom displays and eye-catching teaching materials. Your students can conveniently use the images to complete impressive multicultural projects, book jackets or report covers. Create meaningful original art treasures for your classrooms by combining the images given with the activities suggested, or compare world cultures by relating these images to other cultural crafts and artifacts you've discovered.

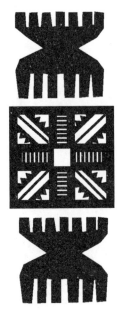

We Are All Artists

We all have things to say in our images and our art. Each artist brings a unique perspective and vision to his or her creations. Artists respect each others' ideas, look for new ways to improve their skills, and take the time to practice and improve their art techniques. Using the images and activities available in this book will enable you and your students to see the expression of art as a process toward growth in individual and group expression, confidence and communication.

Cultural Connections

Although the style of images of world cultures can vary greatly, the reasons for making art are universal. Art symbolizes a culture's history and social values. Art may also communicate traits societies feel are beneficial for a good life such as leadership, honesty, bravery, or patience. Decorating objects, clothing and housewares with animals, flowers, or icons may bring good weather or plentiful rain for bountiful harvests according to some beliefs. Motifs that serve to predict happiness or discourage bad influences are also common. Seasons of the year, religious holidays and important life pas-

sages are celebrated with special artwork. Along with the clip art for each section, we have included information about the culture and the art shown. In some chapters, charts are included to share symbols and their meanings. Seeing how cultures communicate through their art will help your students make positive cultural connections.

Art, Environmentally Speaking

Art forms spring from the abundance of natural materials available to the artist. Each society uses plants from the surrounding area to make some form of paper or cloth. Seeds, gourds, bones, shells, wood and leather are carved, hollowed out, strung, and painted. Pigments derived from plant juices, and minerals are ground to make colored paints, dyes and sand for decorative application. Recognizing and respecting the gifts of the natural world that have enriched our arts will help your students appreciate each culture's geographical treasures, some of which are becoming endangered today, or changing as ancient ways are replaced with modern technology.

The Art of Cultural Exchange

Travel and trade have always influenced the arts. Creative materials such as fabrics, beads, shells, woods, metals, leathers, and dyes have been bartered between cultures for centuries. Not only raw materials, but art styles, images and techniques have been shared as well. People enjoy exchanging materials and ideas while adapting them to their own traditions. Commerce today makes it possible for us to see, enjoy and even purchase arts and crafts from around the world.

Art in Today's World

The place of arts in the world cultures is changing daily. There are many world cultures today that depend solely on their creation of arts and crafts for economic independence and growth. Some arts that were very costly or time consuming to create in the past are now being simplified so that they are more competitive for sale in today's world. Certain styles of art or images that had symbolic meaning may now be created primarily for use as a commercial product. Some traditional art forms disappear as people have no further time or use for them, or may become unavailable as the natural resources needed to make them are depleted. However, new materials and opportunities create new artistic pathways for each society.

Making Art Meaningful

It is our hope that in becoming more aware of the arts and images of world cultures, students can tune into the images and arts in their personal experiences today. Ask your students to relate their own ethnic histories and family arts traditions to some of the art seen here.

Here are some questions you might want to share. What images are significant to our current culture? To students lives personally? What symbols are used to celebrate and call attention to seasonal events? What type of art could be used in your own classroom setting to symbolize positive social outcomes and meanings? Use the images in this collection to enrich your classroom environment and to stimulate your students so that they may begin to discover and share their understanding of how other people live. Encourage your students to copy and clip out art from this book to construct projects, booklets, crafts, wearables, gifts and artifacts of special meaning to them.

USING CLIP ART IN THIS BOOK

Reproduce any of the art in this book for use on research projects, craft activities, decorations, invitations, displays, and stationery in your classroom. Here are some tips to help you and your students use the clip art provided in the collection.

Making Copies

Copy Your Clip Art

Make one or two clean copies of each image you want to use. Do not cut into this volume.

Plan Your Clip Art

- Using a paper cutter to cut the borders will make them easier to position.
- If you are reproducing small items, gang them up on a page to save paper.
- Measure your margin, draw a light pencil line or use a blue grid paper to help position the art.
- Try some of the stationary designs shown below.

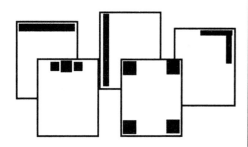

- Copy a page of extra symbols to seal your envelope for a finished touch!

Assembling Your Clip Art

- Mount the art onto your craft pattern, or onto a clean, white paper.
- Use a thin coat of rubber cement, a bit of removable tape, glue stick, adhesive spray or dry mount for a wrinkle-free bond.
- Before copying, remove any excess glue or adhesive from around the image. Glue can attract dust and dirty the print or glass on the copy machine and ruin your final copy.

Choosing Your Copier

- This clip art will reproduce the easiest with a standard copy machine.
- If you do not have access to a standard copy machine, check with your school office to see if you need to prepare your artwork in a special way before using your school's copying equipment.

Testing Your Project

- Make sure the paper you choose can be printed with your machine and works well with the art materials you've selected.
- Test samples can be used to demonstrate your project techniques and will assure your craft is successful.

Reproducing Your Clip Art

- Copy the image onto construction paper, file folder, medium-weight board, or bond paper. If you want something special, look to office supply stores which have bulk paper in many interesting colors and patterns.
- Reproduce the artwork for each student adding extras in case mistakes are made.

Enlarging Art

On a Copy Machine

- Use a copy machine with an enlargement feature if larger copies are desired.
- Depending on the type of machine and enlargement limits, you may need to enlarge art two or three times to reach your goal.
- Make an extra copy of the enlarged sample for your files.

On an Overhead Projector

- For larger displays, copy the image onto a clear transparency, or trace the original image with a fine-tip indelible marker onto a lightweight acetate.
- Place the transparent art onto an overhead projector.
- Project it onto a wall where you have affixed a poster board, or bulletin board-sized craft paper for final tracing and coloring.

Storing Clip Art

Filing Tips
- Keep a clean, spare copy in a file folder for future reference, especially the enlarged copies; to save time later.

Future Activity Folders
- After your activity has been completed, include a sample or snapshot of the craft in this file for future reference.
- Note how the activity worked for your groups and what things you would change for future presentations.

Add to Your Clip Art Collection
- Keep copies of clean, reproducible student drawings. Students might explain and label the country/culture of each of their images.

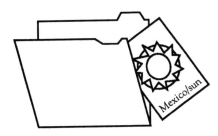

Additional Resources

- If you would like to find more images for a specific country, use the bibliography on page 17 and 18.

Artful Displays

The Texture, Sound and Feel of Other Cultures
- Clip art can be used as patterns for stencils or stamps.
- Drape the fabric on book cases, or over your desk for a softer, warmer feel and interesting look.

- Instead of cardboard boxes and plastic trays, use woven baskets and clay bowls (for older students) to hold pencils, crayons, etc.
- Use music from other cultures as "mood music".

Cultural Classroom Accents
- Use the clip art images to create borders, or decorative flourishes on cupboards, doorways, or other areas of your room.

More Classroom Accents
- Code your classroom duty charts with some of the symbols seen here.
- Instead of name tags, have your students choose a piece of art to cut and tape to their desk to call it home.
- Surround your students with decorative images to engage them in a new cultural awarenesses.

Big, Bigger, Biggest Displays
- Enlarge designs to make wallpaper for your bulletin boards.

Divide and Conquer
- Turn a folded piece of cardboard into an oriental screen or room divider by decorating it with colorful pieces of clip art.

- Create culture carrels by using the clip art to decorate book cases or larger study corners.

Teacher's Guide

Holiday Helps
- Use the images for quick copy and cut out ornaments for multicultural holiday displays.
- Clip art can be used for invitations, borders and decorations when learning about holiday celebrations or displays around the world.
- Use the chart below to note any special events or holiday dates from other cultures as a reminder for future classroom planning.

Cultural Inspirations
- Borrow cultural objects from friends or students to set up a cultural display. Use the display for children to sketch from, or write stories about when they have free time.

Cultural Discoveries
- Set up a special display with an Art Mystery of the Week. This can be a sample of clip art, or a three-dimensional object. Ask children to identify what it is, where it came from, and what it was used for. Local museums may be helpful in giving you tips for challenging art or objects to include.

Culture in Your Classroom
- Display all the children's activities with special flair by creating posters or frames from enlarged pages from the stationery section. Or, decorate construction paper with clip art borders. Celebrating your student's individual cultural identities is the best way to encourage an appreciation of cultural diversity.

Country	Holiday	Date	Clip Art

PROJECTS AND ACTIVITIES

We have named specific clip art with which to try the following activities, but we encourage you to experiment with other pieces, too! Make note of others to use in the space provided for future reference!

Cultural Learning Through Art

Choose clip art images from the culture you want to study. Mount them on cards for display. Ask your students (individually or in groups) to choose an image that appeals to them and make inferences about the cultures they represent. What is pictured? Why was it made? What materials made it? After you have discussed the pictures, look to other resources to round out their knowledge of the culture represented in the scene.

Suggested Clip Art: Any selection can be used.

Guiding Cultural Art Discoveries

Divide a paper into 9 squares. Reduce a small piece of art for each square and give to the students when you are planning a field trip to a museum or art gallery. Have the students look for examples of similar art, or find out more information about the culture that the art represents. Ask your students to share their discoveries!

Suggested Clip Art: Any selection can be used.

Cultural Enrichment Through Art

When you complete a story or unit, ask students to choose and copy clip art images that best fit the culture you just studied. Ask them to create a display that makes use of the art and gives additional information about each culture.

Suggested Clip Art: Any selection can be used.

Stamp It!

Choose simple 2" x 3" (or smaller) images to create hand-made stamps. Note: With any of these methods, the image will appear in reverse. On some designs this will not matter. If it needs to print as shown, turn the copy over and trace it from the back before you begin the process.

Potato Stamp

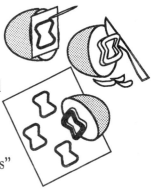

Cut the potato in half. Hold the pattern on the bottom of the potato, and prick around the edges of the design with a sharp toothpick. Remove the paper and "follow the dots" to cut out the around the image using a plastic knife. Take off the white part of the image and leave the black as a raised imprint on the potato. Use tempera or acrylic paints to stamp the images onto paper, pieces of cloth, or articles of clothing. Repeat the images in neatly spaced blocks to mimic African Adinkra textiles and South Pacific tapa cloths.

Suggested Clip Art: African Adinkra art, page 23.

Other:_____

Rubber Stamp

Trace the pattern as previously mentioned onto the front of a rubber eraser, and cut away the black line, so that the imprint looks as if it prints in reverse. These can be alternated with the potato stamp imprints and used similarly.

Suggested Clip Art: Swaziland art, page 32. (use simpler patterns)

Other:_____

Raised Impressions

Glue the clip art to a piece of cardboard. Use a whole-page design, or glue a number of small images to make a whole page. Trace the black lines with a thick line of glue. Let dry. To print, use a roller coated with a water-based ink to distribute color evenly over the tops of the raised glue designs. Place a sheet of paper on top, and use a clean roller (or your fingers lightly pressing) to print the inked images onto the paper. Chalk or crayon rubbings can also be made from the plate.

Suggested Clip Art: Peruvian symbols, page 80.
Other:_____

Pierced Art

Choose 3"- 6" designs and use the punching technique (that you used on the potato stamp) to transfer your image onto medium-weight paper. Experiment with a sharp pencil lead, ball point pen, or the tip of a knitting needle to see what works best with your paper and the design you chose. Place the design over a sheet of construction paper over a corrugated board or sheet of styrofoam, so the holes poke through well. Wrap in a cylinder and hang with paper streamers for a lantern, or wrap top on a dowel and hang straight in the window.

Suggested Clip Art: Indian art, page 45.
Other:_____

Cutting Edge Artwork

Many cultures have used cut-paper in their festival finery and arts. Any simple design can be adapted for a cut paper project by following these guidelines: Note: To make the activities easier for younger children, enlarge the clip art before using.

Folded-Paper Cut Outs

Choose a symmetrical design. Divide the art in half and cut apart. The cut edge will be placed along the folded paper edge. Use removable tape or paper clips to hold in place while the outline of the design is traced with carbon onto the paper below. Remove the pattern and cut along the lines of the design. Refer to your pattern frequently as you cut, removing the parts of the design which are white, and leaving the black areas of design. When cutting is complete, open carefully. Color can be added to the design by "filling in the holes" by gluing or taping small pieces of colored paper behind some of the areas on the back of the design, or adding rosettes or leaves to the front of the design. Mount your finished piece onto construction paper.

Suggested Clip Art: Polish art, page 55.
Other:_____

Openwork Paper Cutting

Any simple, non-symmetrical scene or figure can be chosen. Note: This activity is recommended for older students who can handle sharp scissors easier. A thin coat of rubber cement on back side of the pattern (art) piece can be used to tack it temporarily to a piece of colored paper. Cut out the white areas and leave the black areas as before. When the cutting is done, peel off the pattern, leaving the colored cut paper design. Mount the design on a contrasting paper and trim.

Suggested Clip Art: Inuit art, page 114.
Other:_____

Artful Fans or Banners

Cut openwork or folded paper designs. Place between two wax paper sheets. Sandwich thin rods of wood between the layers. Use a warm iron with a protective sheet under it it to gently fuse the art inside the wax paper. Trim the wax paper to make different shaped fans as shown. To make banners, use the same technique with rectangles of paper, wrapping the top and bottom edge onto wooden dowels.

Suggested Clip Art: Japanese art, page 50.
Other_____

Decorative Decals

Attach trimmed clip art images by applying painted layers of thinned white glue or acrylic gloss medium to decoupage cut images onto drums, bowls, plaques, or boxes.

Suggested Clip Art: Swedish motifs, page 63.
Other:_____

Mosaic

Mount enlarged clip art to a cardboard or tag board base. Glue tiny cut paper pieces to fill in the white areas inside the image, or fill in the white areas with gray or clay-colored paint to be "grout" and place colored pieces on the black areas of the drawings. Other mosaic materials might be colored egg shells, fish tank gravel, rice, macaroni or seeds.

Suggested Clip Art: Arabic art, page 82.
Other:_____

Cut Paper Appliqué

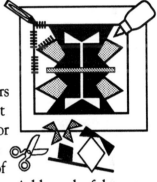

Enlarge a clip art panel with lots of detail. Copy the scene on various colors of construction paper. Cut the figures out of one color to glue onto another base or make up a new scene of your own on another color. Add a colorful paper border to the edge. Make each piece look "stitched" by adding fine lines with crayon or markers after all pieces have been glued in place.

Suggested Clip Art: Native American art, page 105.
Other:_____

Colorful Techniques

Crayon Resist

Place your clip art design under a piece of plain white copy paper. Trace the design in yellow or white. Add lines of textures to fill in areas. When you are done, paint over the entire sheet with black, dark blue or dark brown. Trim paper about 1" from edge of design and mount on a bright colored piece of construction paper.

Suggested Clip Art: Aboriginal art, page 88.
Other:_____

Crayon Iron-Transfer

Place your clip art design under a piece of plain white copy paper. Trace the design in bright, waxy crayon colors. When complete, turn design over and iron onto a shirt or a piece of fabric. Note: The design will come out reverse! There are special crayons formulated for fabric application available.
Suggested Clip Art: Egyptian art, page 19.
Other:_____

Stencils

Copy your design onto tag board. Cut away the black areas of the design and use the black piece for sponge-printing or chalk-rubbing negative stencil patterns.
If you wish, use the outside part of the design for positive stenciling with brushes or sponges.
Suggested Clip Art: South Pacific art, page 91.
Other:_____

Sand Painting

Choose a round clip art motif. Glue your clip art to cardboard. Use glue to trace the outlines of the design and sprinkle with sand. Colored sand is now available for crafts like these. Note: Special clean, white silica sand can be purchased locally, but cornmeal or salt can also be used. Pizza cardboards work great, and can also be purchased at nominal cost from vendors.
Suggested Clip Art: Hopi motifs, page111.
Other:_____

Artistic Overlays

Clip art designs can be used as a convenient base to which a variety of craft materials can be glued. Tacky glue works best on all types of materials. Copy or trace your design onto a cardboard base so that it will not buckle with the weight of the glue and overlays.

Straw Art

Straw can be purchased from farmers or garden stores. Use straw as a round stalk, or split, soaked in water (to soften) and flattened, pressed and dried. Corn husks can also be used in place of straw. Cut into 1" or shorter lengths and glue over the open areas of the design in neat, side to side patterns. The direction of the rows of straw will add a lovely texture to the simple drawings. When designs are complete, the surrounding art area can be filled in with marker or painted dark brown or black.
Suggested Clip Art: Belorussian art, page 54.
Other:_____

Yarn Paintings

Traditional yarn paintings are made with a layer of beeswax on a board into which yarn is pressed. For your classroom, use clip art mounted on cardboard. Glue the outlines first, then fill in the yarn in a row by row fashion. Start on the outside and fill in each area in turn. Use bright, almost fluorescent colors to make bold designs.
Suggested Clip Art: Panama mola art, page 76.
Other:_____

Indian Mirror Embroidery

The traditional art is done with tiny mirrors fastened with embroidery thread onto cloth. For your classroom, cut small pieces of shiny foil to glue onto parts of the clip art designs. Outline the outside of each symbol in bright colors of yarn, or raised fabric paints. Areas next to the foil can be "shisha stitched" (small stitches like the edge of a buttonhole) with a permanent pen that matches the yarn color, or with the fabric paint.

Suggested Clip Art: Indian art, page 45.
Other:_____

Multicultural Storytelling and Puppetry

Legends, fables, holiday stories and religious beliefs are told through puppets in many cultures. Clip art can help you recreate some of them.

Kachina Dancers

Copy the clip art on heavier board. Draw a body below the head. Cut out. Color the figure and add a flat wooden stick at the top behind the head, so that the dolls can be held above and skipped across the ground as if to "dance."
Tape a strip of border clip art into a circle to make a "stage." Kachina-type dolls are traditionally colored in 6 basic colors for their 6 directions: yellow = north, blue-green = west, red = south, white = east, grey = above, black = below.

Suggested Clip Art: Hopi Sun Kachina art, page 111.
Other:_____

Shadow Dancers

Known as Wayang Kulit, these are jointed puppets that have long sticks attached from the bottom. Glue the puppet clip art onto tag board. Color each piece. Use the traditional colors of gold, black, white, yellow, red or blue. Fashion a shadow dancer screen by suspending an old white sheet or thin white paper in a doorway or from a board between two desks. Tape a small flashlight to a book or box to shine on the screen, just behind the puppeteer. The puppeteer (Dalang) recites a story to accompany the puppets, and music, gongs and drums accompany the performance.

Suggested Clip Art: Indian puppets, page 45.
Other:_____

Myth Masks

Use the clip art designs to create colorful masks to wear while you recite or perform traditional myths and stories of many cultures. Glue the clip art to tag board and add painted accents, raffia, feathers, yarn, and beads. Create costumes to go with each mask, using bright colors such as gold, red, black, green yellow and blue.

Suggested Clip Art: Northwest Coast art, page 113.
Other:_____

Folk Tale Finishes

Use clip art motifs to create artistic accents or moveable characters for folk tales from different lands. Enlarge onto colorful construction paper to create a shaped cover for a story book. Reduce images to make finger puppets to go along with oral stories. Use as spots of art, or repeat as borders in hand printed tales of your own.

Suggested Clip Art: Russian animal art, page 60.
Other_____

Artful Wearables

Hand-painted Beads

Copy tiny copies of the clip art symbols onto wooden beads, or hand-made air dry clay beads with a small brush and acrylic paint.

Suggested Clip Art: Chinese symbols, page 34.
Other:_____

Necklaces

String the hand-made beads alone knotting the string between beads, or alternate with (purchased) small glass or wooden beads. Glue any of the smaller clip art motifs to a heavy cardboard base and cut out to create an amulet to hand from the necklace. Use string, tiny seed beads, or glue swirls to add texture to the design surface. Note: Coordinate motifs to be repeated in the amulet and beads as shown.

Suggested Clip Art: Scandinavian motifs, page 53.
Other:_____

Bangle Bracelets

Copy some of the borders and panels of clip art onto red, brown, or yellow construction paper. Make a number of copies of each to wrap. Cut one 3" x 8" tag board strip for each bracelet. To fit your arm, add 1" extra, and trim. Wrap the strips of patterns onto the tag board as shown. Overlap 1/2" and glue. Coat bracelet with thinned glue or acrylic gloss medium to make it durable and shiny.

Suggested Clip Art: Native American designs, page 107.
Other:

_____

Paper Beadery

Copy some of the textured panels of clip art onto red, brown, or yellow construction paper. Cut into the strip shapes shown and wrap around a pencil from the wide part to the tip. Secure the end with a dab of glue, then coat the whole bead with thinned glue or acrylic gloss medium to make them durable and shiny. Repeat the process for the number of beads you would like. Enlarge strip pattern for biggger beads.

Suggested Clip Art: African cloth, page 31.
Other:

_____

Artful Bags

Copy the clip art pattern onto brown craft paper. Add more colors to the design by tracing with crayons or markers along areas of the designs. Fold the panel in half, and glue the sides together to form a pocket. Cut cords to glue or tie to the top to make a handle or strap.

Suggested Clip Art:
South Pacific art, page 91. (use larger panel at bottom)

Other:_____

Artful Headgear

Enlarge clip art to make decorative panels to wear as headdresses. Decorate your own hat patterns or hat shapes or purchase head bands to attach strips or medallions of clip art. Use tagboard for durability. Test sizes and patterns for fit before attaching clip art.

Suggested Clip Art: Hmong art, page 39 and 40.

Other:_____

Headgear Styles:

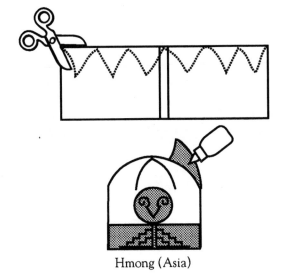

Hmong (Asia)

Headgear Styles:

Ghana (Africa)

Thailand (Asia)

head band

Burmese
(India)

Hopi
(Native American)

Artful Playthings

Kites (For display only)

Enlarge the clip art to 11" x 17" size paper. Lay a piece of tissue over the clip art. Trace the lines onto tissue paper with a black marker and cut out along the outside edge. Create a framework for the kite to be glued onto. Tie string on the end 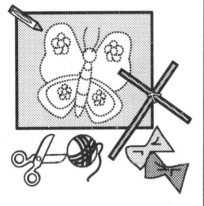 an add tissue paper ties from the edge of the kite to the end. Layers of tissue can be added here and there to accent the design.

Suggested Clip Art: Mexican butterfly, page 72.
Other:_____

Kites (For flying)

Purchase a kite pattern and trace it onto lightweight white paper. Draw the motif as seen and color with markers. Use the framework from the original kite on your model. Follow the manufacturer's directions to fly kite.

Suggested Clip Art: Japanese art, page 48.
Other:_____

Games

Clip art can be used to create a number of games from many cultures. Research the type of game you would like to create,  then find appropriate art to decorate or create game pieces such as sticks, dice, or grids.

Suggested Clip Art: Any clip art can be used.

Dolls

Russians use straw to make dolls. Native Americans use corn husks. Mexicans use papier mâché. Try some of these crafts to make multicultural dolls. Even simple paper dolls are fun! Use the patterns in the book as fabric to copy, color and cut out belts, dresses or skirts for your dolls. The ethnic sketches below might give you some ideas of how to dress your dolls.

Suggested Clip Art: Any clip art can be used.

Clothing Styles:

South America

India

Africa

China

Japan

Middle East

Middle East

Russia

Stemmer House Resources

We would like to extend our thanks to Barbara Holdridge at Stemmer House Publishers for making some of their fine quality drawings available for use in this book. To expand your clip art library, use the following bibliography to purchase these titles featuring complete collections of clip art. The Stemmer House series; International Design Library books are available at art or book stores, or send for a complete catalog at **Stemmer House Publishers, Inc. 2627 Caves Road, Owings Mill, Maryland 21117.**

1. *African Designs of the Guinea Coast* illustrated by Caren Caraway, designed by Barbara Holdridge ©1985 Stemmer House Publishers
Art used in this book:
African Guinea Coast art (page 25)
African Guinea Coast cloth (page 26)

2. *African Designs of the Nigeria and the Cameroons* illustrated by Caren Caraway, designed by Barbara Holdridge ©1986 Stemmer House Publishers
Art used in this book:
African Nigerian art (three)(page 27, 28)
African Cameroon circle motifs (four)(page 29)

3. *African Designs of the Congo* illustrated by Caren Caraway, designed by Barbara Holdridge ©1986 Stemmer House Publishers
Art used in this book:
Bateke African shield (page 30)
Bushongo African carving (page 30)
Bangba African tapestry (page 31)

4. *Hmong Textile Designs* illustrated by Anthony Chan, designed by Barbara Holdridge ©1990 Stemmer House Publishers
Art used in this book:
Hmong folkstory cloth with water dragon (page 42)
Hmong folkstory cloth with bird family (page 42)
Hmong flower cloth with symbolic patterns (six)(page 43)

5. *Traditional Chikankari Embroidery Patterns of India* illustrated by Pradumma and Rosalba Tana, designed by Barbara Holdridge ©1984 Stemmer House Publishers
Art used in this book:
Chikankari embroidery designs (page 44)
Chikankari embroidery designs (page 45)
Chikankari embroidery designs (page 23)
Chikankari embroidery designs (page 27)

6. *Ancient Scandinavian Designs* illustrated by Bev Ulsrud Van Berkom, designed by Barbara Holdridge ©1985 Stemmer House Publishers
Art used in this book:
Ancient Scandinavian picture stones (two)(page 52)
Ancient Scandinavian Borre art (page 52)
Ancient Scandinavian Urnes art (page 52)

7. *Folk Art Designs* illustrated by Ramona Jablonski, designed by Barbara Holdridge ©1978 Stemmer House Publishers
Art used in this book:
Polish cut paper wedding scene (page 58)
Polish cut paper rooster (page 58)

8. *Spanish Ceramic Designs* illustrated by Anita Benarde, designed by Barbara Holdridge ©1981 Stemmer House Publishers
Art used in this book:
Spanish border, plate and two tiles (page 62)

9. *Aztec and other Mexican Indian Designs* illustrated by Caren Caraway, designed by Barbara Holdridge ©1984 Stemmer House Publishers
Art used in this book:
Ancient Mexican eagle, figure, animal symbol and bird symbols (page 67)

10. *The Mayan Design Book* illustrated by Caren Caraway, designed by Barbara Holdridge ©1981 Stemmer House Publishers
Art used in this book:
Mayan bird and serpent Dresden codex figure (page 69)
Mayan jaguar figure (page 69)
Mayan priest, cocoa pod bowl design (plage 69)
Mayan winged figure clay plate (page 70)
Mayan 560 AD ball player & game marker panel (page 70)
Mayan jaguar with human heart carved relief panel (page 70)

11. *The Mola Design Book* illustrated by Caren Caraway, designed by Barbara Holdridge ©1981 Stemmer House Publishers
Art used in this book:
Mola with fish (page 76)
Mola with cat (page 77, 78)
Mola with turtles (page 77, 78)
Mola with birds/fish (page 77)
Mola with alligator (page 78)

12. *Hawaiian and Easter Island Designs* illustrated by Caren Caraway, designed by Barbara Holdridge ©1989 Stemmer House Publishers
Art used in this book:
Hawaiian kapa-spana cloth designs (three)(page 93)

Stemmer House Resources / Bibliography

13. **South Pacific Designs** illustrated by Caren Caraway, designed by Barbara Holdridge ©1981 Stemmer House Publishers
Art used in this book:
New Guinea designs (three)(page 99)
Solomon Island carving (page 99)

14. **Northwest Indian Designs** illustrated by Caren Caraway, designed by Barbara Holdridge ©1982 Stemmer House Publishers
Art used in this book:
Northwest Tlingit bear chilkat blanket (page 112)
Northwest Haida shark painting (page 112)
Northwest Tsimshian bear painted house (page 112)
Northwest Kwakiutl raven canoe (page 113)

The following books are recommended resources for cultural crafts and activities:

1. **Crafts of Many Cultures: 30 Authentic Craft Projects from Around the World** by Aurelia Gomez (Scholastic Professional Books, 1993)

2. **Brown Bag Ideas from Many Cultures** by Irene Tejada (Davis Publications,1993)

3. **Art from Many Hands: Multicultural Art Projects for Home and School** by Jo Miles Schuman (Prentice-Hall, Inc. 1981)

4. **Multi-Cultural Art Projects** by Vera Jo Groswold and Judith Starke (Love Publishing Company, 1980)

5. **Multicultural Art Activities from the Cultures of Africa, Asia, and North America** written by Darlene Ritter, illustrated by Diane Valko, edited by Judy Urban (Creative Teaching Press, 1993)

6. **Multicultural Fables and Fairy Tales: Stories and Activities to Promote Literacy and Cultural Awareness** by Tara McCarthy (Scholastic Professional Books, 1993)

7. **World Crafts** by Jacqueline Herald (Lark Books, 1992)

8. Ancient and Living Cultures Stencil series:
• **Pueblo Indians and the Southwest**
• **Ancient Celts**
• **Northwest Coast Indians**
• **Ancient Mexico**
• **West Africa: Ghana**
by Big World: Mira Bartók and Christine Ronan (Good Year Books, 1993)

9. **Magic Symbols of the World** by Pearl Binder (Hamlyn Publishing Group, Ltd., 1972)

Ancient Egyptian

Egyptian art was highly stylized, and used generously on wall paintings, tombs, temples and to decorate everyday objects. Figures were drawn in strict poses, with body positon and clothing having symbolic significance. Animal and plant figures had religious meaning and were connected with natural forces. Gods or magical dieties are shown as figures with animal heads, or animals with human heads. Stylized plants such as papyrus, palmetto, and lotus were used repeatedly, as well as the sun and moon, cobras, sacred cows and scarabs. Sacred writing called hieroglyphs could be read as picture-words, names or captions, or could convey important beliefs in addition to the art.

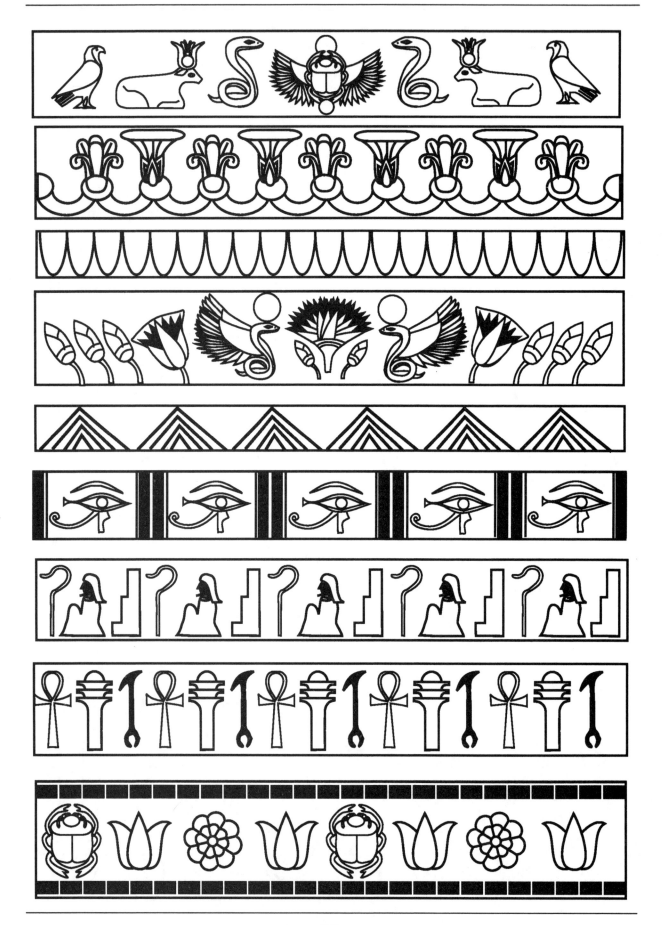

Ancient Egyptian

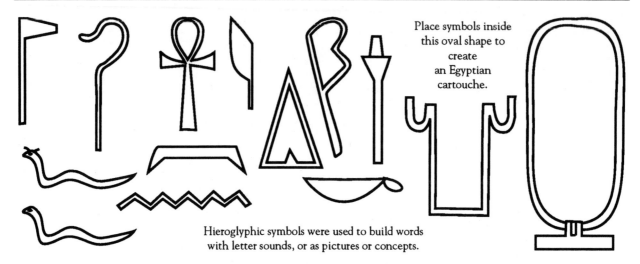

Place symbols inside this oval shape to create an Egyptian cartouche.

Hieroglyphic symbols were used to build words with letter sounds, or as pictures or concepts.

vulture: short a sound

crown of lower Egypt

God

goodness, beauty and joy (nefer)

basket: letter k sound

symbol for life (anch)

flowering reed: short i sound

owl: letter m sound

crown of upper Egypt

God

cartouche: contained names of gods or kings

heart (ib)

truth and justice (maat)

water: letter n sound

feathers: eternity

falcon: God Horus

double crown

throne

eternity (djed)

snake: letters "adj" sound

horned viper: letter "f" sound

symbol for "to give"

horizon

crown of Sun Goddess Hathor

udjat eye: health and happiness

sceptre symbol for "to rule" (heka)

sceptre showing well-being (was)

sky

ka: immortal substance (soul)

sceptre symbol for power

North Africa

African art from Ghana, Guinea Coast, Nigeria and the Cameroons feature fabrics, appliqué work, and carvings that show the bold and energetic images typical of North African art. Ghanian *Adinkra* cloth symbols reflect important values and traditions that have been shared for generations. A grid-like panel, created for special occasions, may tell a story, a proverb, or give special blessings to the wearer. The fertile forests of the Guinea Coast are reflected in art filled with bold geometric patterns of woven cloth and animals, birds, fishes and plants appliquéd onto circular panels. Nigeria has developed many styles of art but most are done for religious reasons. Animals and birds typical of that area are shown in rich carved relief. East of Nigeria, art and artists of the Cameroons are also highly esteemed. Included are intricately detailed appliqués from one of their four style regions.

Ghana

North Africa

Ghana

most important adinkra

ram's horns: strength

safe house: security

purity

humility

link or chain: relationships

heart: patience and endurance

ladder: death

forgiveness

harmony and unity

fern: defiance

handcuffs: law and slavery

living tree

royalty or King

sanctity and good fortune

seeds: growth

the universe

lock: law and order, authority

moon and stars: faithfulness

hourglass drum

star: dependence

moon: love and kindness

courage

comb: protection

Guinea Coast

Guinea Coast

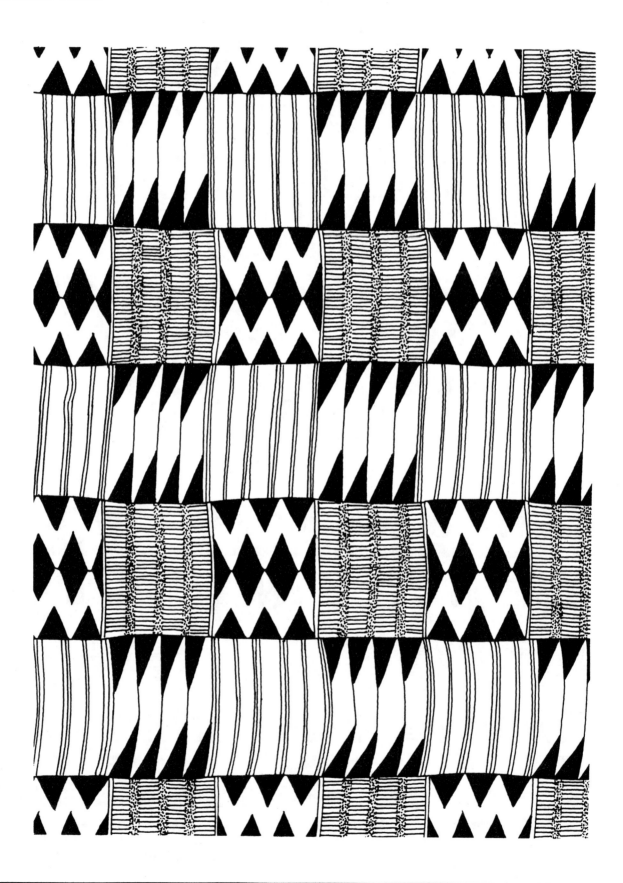

Nigeria

Nigeria

Cameroon

South Africa

African art from various kingdoms in Congo and the Swaziland regions of Africa show an energy-filled attention to abstract design. The Bateke artists of the Congo live in the savannah and create highly revered masks in patterns of red, black and white. In another kingdom in the Congo, Bushongo artisans show a great love of patterned detail in their carvings. Much further south, Swaziland artists make large coiled baskets from local grasses which are dyed and bound in abstract patterns inspired by the world around; the swirling wind, wings of a bird, or leaf-like or floral motifs. General african symbols at the end of this section illustrate bold abstract motifs typical of African folk tales, decoration and myths.

Congo

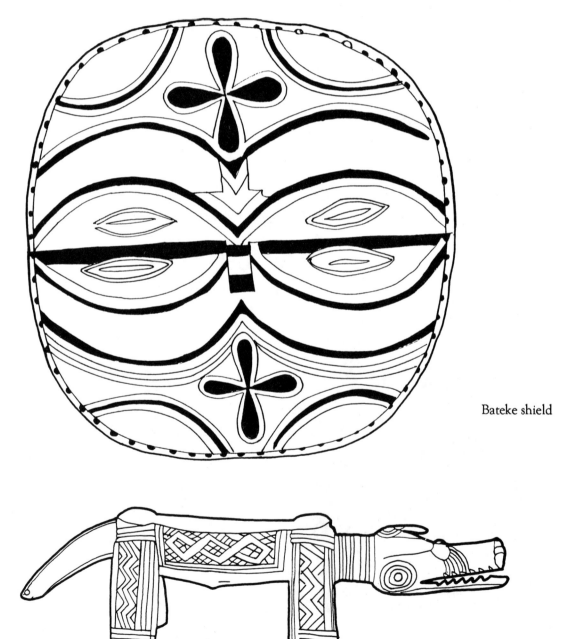

Bateke shield

Bushongo carving

Congo

Bangba cloth

Swaziland

Africa

China

The Chinese artist's palette uses the beauty of nature, the seasons of the year and every season of a person's life from birth to old age. The crossed paths, or gammadion symbol (two versions below) is often seen and symbolizes the four directions plus center; the human race. The Lotus flower symbol, signifying marriage, is very evident in their art. Every part of this highly prized plant is used by the Chinese culture; the roots make cooling beverages, the leaves are used to cover food in cooking, the flowers are used for decoration and to make fragrances. Chinese surround themselves with beauty; lacy wooden latticework panels adorn palaces and homes, pairs of protective animal figurines stand guard at doorways and gates, and rich embroidered fabrics and tapestries are covered with motifs featuring nature symbols from every season.

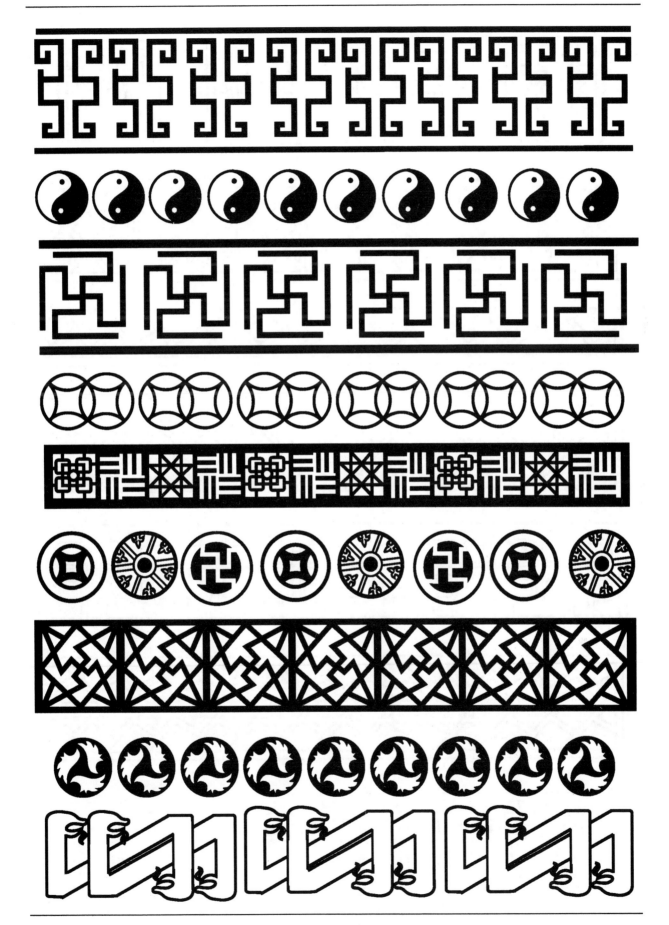

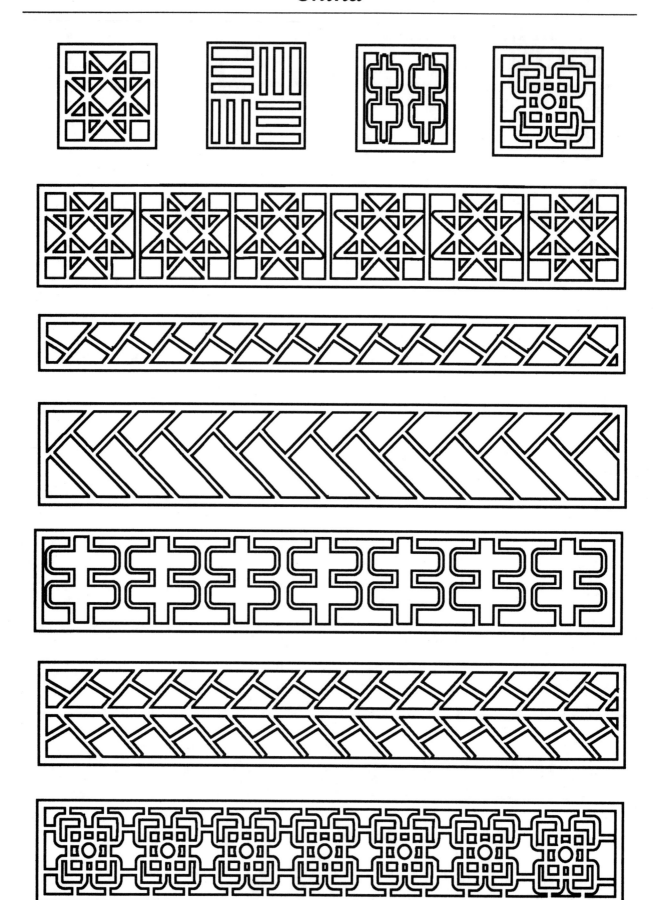

China

Symbols and their Meanings

human race

shell: victory (lo)

moon (ch'ien)

dragon (lung)

pine: immortality

peony: spring

lotus: marriage

fish: abundance (yu)

balance and harmony
(yin-yang)

spinning wheel:
law (lun)

chrysanthemum:
joy in retirement

good luck

sun (chu)

three stars (hsing chen)

cloud and thunder symbol

Hmong

The artwork of Southeast Asia is rich in symbolic imagery and symmetry. Until 1950, the Hmong (one of the hill tribes of S.E. Asia, many of whom now live in the U.S.) did not have a written language; their culture has been passed along through songs, stories and stitched panels called flower and story cloths. Flower cloths have symbolic shapes with geometric patterns similar to these below. Story cloths use simple animal shapes and tell family histories and cultural myths. Both are very precise with a variety of colors, layers of fabric and tiny stitches. Other tribes use similar patterns to cross-stitch onto clothing and hats or woven fabrics. Recreate some of the designs to create beautifully crafted flower and story cloth originals!

Hmong

Symbols and their Meanings

8-pointed star: good luck

dogfoot

home: powerful
good spirits

elephant foot: great wealth

snail shell: growth of family

dragon tail: good health

mountains, scales,
teeth: protection

waterlily

heart

centipede: healing medicine

tortoise:
most truthful messenger

clamshell

fireworks: celebration

cucumber seed

ram's head

stair steps

pinwheel

India

The art of India is influenced by Hindu and Buddhist traditions, making the elephant and horse very important symbols in their art. Harmonious curved lines and trellis-type lines, flowers and leaves are found in Indian embroidery. One type, the *chikankari*, is stitched with white threads onto white cloth. Another type of embroidery features bright threads accented with glittery mirrors. Artistic expression is highly valued, and even doorways are adorned with simple parrot and leaf designs in colored sand to welcome guests. Important symbols are hand-stitched into a patchwork-type cloth called *kantha* for gifts and family occasions. Art traditions are used for recreation, too. Adults and children enjoy puppet plays starring artfully crafted hand-made puppets called *wayant kulit*.

India

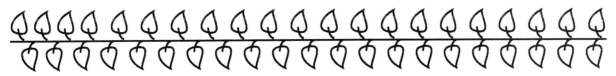

Symbols and their Meanings

sacred elephant:
remover of obstacles

wheel: plenty

mandala (lotus shape):
universe

parrot: hospitality

winnowing fan: plenty

horse: power

tree of life:
four directions of wind and
four phases of life

fish: plenty

Japan

Japanese have a great tradition of respect and reverence for nature. Trees, mountains, water, gardens, birds and flowers are used, and are similar to Chinese art, but designed in a more stylized fashion. The beauty of nature is condensed and simplified into strong design elements that are repeated in fabrics, screens and on paintings. Ancient symbols once used as family crests on helmets, banners and armor are now used as textile designs and to advertise Japanese products.

Symbols and their Meanings

tortoise: long life

carp (koi):
strength and bravery

crane: long life,
happiness, good marriage

dragonfly: summer

cherry blossom: national
flower, life's fleeting moments

butterfly:
temporary beauty

wave (nami): life and
destruction

bamboo (take):
strength and flexibility

Ancient Scandinavian

The ancient Nordic peoples enjoyed the art of rich embellishment on their boats, houses, weapons, jewelry and even horse's gear. Vines and tendrils were popular in Europe, but they favored fantastic, mysterious bird and animals forms. Vikings also quickly absorbed things of interest from other cultures. They combined Roman coin images with Nordic horses and other fertility symbols into abstract-style amulets. Besides valuing the intricate beauty of their subjects, they believed the spirit of the figures rested in their art. Ancient writing called *runes* were used in their artwork as magical charms. Their art represented and encouraged protection, discovery, fellowship and adventure.

Ancient Scandinavian

Scandinavian picture stone

Scandinavian Urnes art

Scandinavian Borre art

Scandinavian picture stone

Symbols and their Meanings

	Nordic runic alphabet						
Norse symbol for wealth	F a	Þ th	R r	Y k	* h	↑ n	I i	↑ j
Norse symbol for irresistibility	∩ u	Γ f	↑ s	↑ t	B b	Y m	Γ l	Ψ R

Belarus

The city of Zhlobin in Belarus is famous for developing the art of straw inlay. Many of these traditional designs can be found in museum shops and import stores. The designs are based on traditional motifs that include geometric designs, birds, animals and people doing domestic chores.

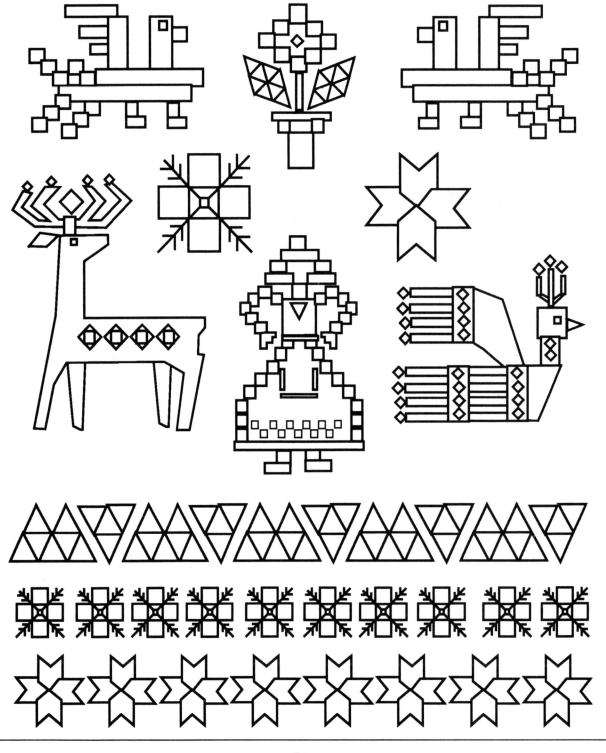

Poland

Polish cottages were filled with imaginative flowers. Brightly colored designs were painted on bowls, ceramics, chests, cottage walls; embroidered into linens and clothing; and carved into wooden shutters. Paper cutting called *wycinaki* expressed their free-wheeling creative spirit and skill in intricate, symmetrical layered designs. Some designs were cut in tiny shapes to decorate eggs for Easter (like the Ukranian *psanky* motifs on page 61) or to hang on the Christmas tree. Other favorite themes in Polish art include farm animals; especially the rooster which symbolizes rebirth and good luck.

Russia

Animal symbols are used frequently in Russian art. Lions symbolize princely generosity and protection. Mythical beasts and birds of many kinds have fantastic wings, tails and other embellishments. The *griffin*, a creature with a lion's body and eagles head and wings, is a traditional symbol for valor and honor. Painted lacquerware is a popular art technique. Wooden boxes and trays are coated with a black shiny finish, then painted with scenes depicting folk tales with very decorative floral details. Russians also hand-paint wooden housewares, musical instruments and toys, too; but in simpler floral and folk motifs.

Spain

Spanish ceramics have rich colors that range from blue, blue green, iridescent green, purplish blue to bright orange red. Although the colors used are distinctly unique to Spain, the patterns and shapes painted on the tiles, pots, plates and other commonly used objects reflect a mix of cultural influences. When the Moors invaded Spain they brought their love of floral and leaf motifs, also seen in Persian, Russian, Turkish and Arabic art.

Sweden

Swedish farm houses are brightened with many decorative arts. Linens and bedding are embroidered, and boxes and kitchen utensils are richly carved. Traditionally, it was the custom of each family to have a set of wooden, hand-carved cookie stamps to use for special holiday celebrations. Brides were given a stamp by her groom, and patterns stayed in families for generations. Stamps included heart, floral and sometimes animal motifs.

Ukraine

Pysanky is a favorite art in the Ukraine. The egg was once a symbol of the life-giving sun, so every spring, Ukranian women celebrate by decorating eggs using the brightest colors they can find from plants, bark and berries. Traditional pysanky symbols are used with present day meanings. The symbols are drawn in lines of melted beeswax onto an egg with a tool called a *kistka*. Intricate patterns are drawn and dyed one section at a time. When complete, wax lines are gently melted and removed to leave the bold colored sections and outlines. Each design is unique; the exact placement of the symbols is never repeated. Note: Pysanky are for gifts and decoration; solid colored eggs called *krashanky* are made to be eaten Easter morning!

Symbols and their Meanings

sun: life and growth

ram: spring life

wheat:
bountiful harvest

butterfly: good health

hen: fertility

pussywillows: spring life

flower:
love and good will

evergreens:
eternal youth and health

sun or star:
life and growth

fish: Christianity

deer: eternal youth
and health

Aztec

The art of the Aztec includes intricate drawings of hieroglyphic images that picture animals, nature and weather symbols. Powerful images show figures of their rulers and Gods rigidly posed in ceremonial postions wearing extravagant costumes and headdresses. Stone carvings, fine gold jewelry, and colorful featherwork and weavings communicate the mysteries and meanings of this highly disciplined and complex society.

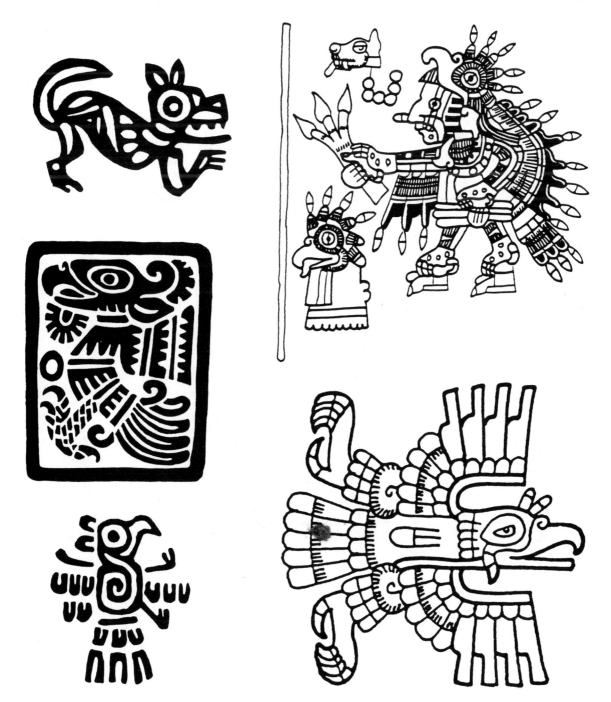

Aztec

Symbols and their Meanings

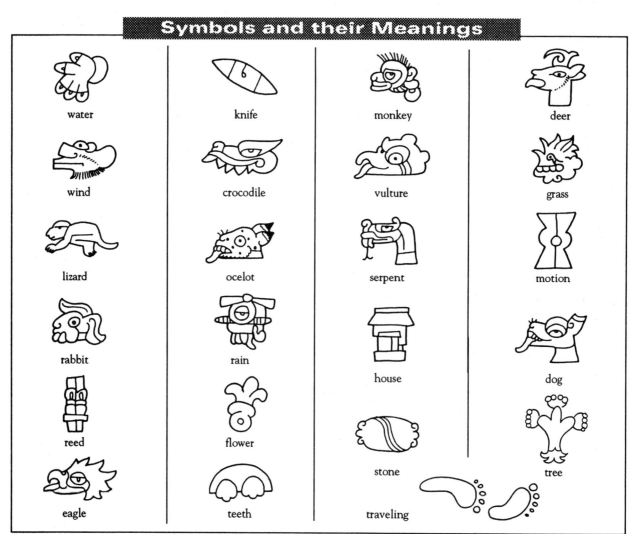

water	knife	monkey	deer
wind	crocodile	vulture	grass
lizard	ocelot	serpent	motion
rabbit	rain	house	dog
reed	flower	stone	tree
eagle	teeth	traveling	

Maya

The art of the Maya included ornate carved stone steles, clay figurines and vessels, engraved jade and shells, and sacred books called *codices*. Intricate scenes of sports, warfare and trade give us an insight into typical activities of the culture and its commerce. Hieroglyphic symbols (ancient versions adapted by the Aztec) decorated calendars and astrological horoscopes. Even the human body was an object of art; elongated skulls, sharply pointed, filed teeth, scars, tattoos, and ear and nose piercing were considered signs of beauty. You can see these features on some of the figures included in this section.

Mexico

Mexican artisans fill their art with abundant decorations that include fantastic nature scenes with lavish details and symmetrical geometric designs. The sun, the most popular symbol in Mexico, is used because it's rays symbolize the cardinal points, rotation of time and the universe. Animals are cut and colored out of tinware for ornaments and display. Magical two and four-headed animals, and figures appear on cut-paper images on *amate* paper, a bark paper similar to those made in Africa and Polynesia. Fantastic flowers and birds are sculpted in earthenware and painted on *amate* bark. Curling, stair-step patterns and stylized birds are used in Mexican borders, and fabrics.

Cut-out amate figures and birds

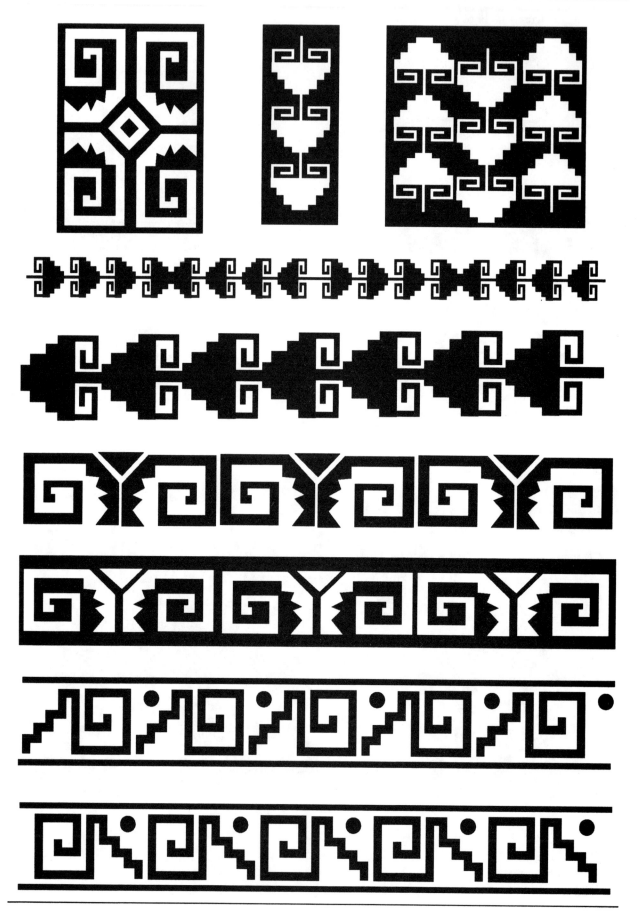

Panama

Mola is a revered fabric art of the women of the Kuna Tribe of Panama. Based on animals, sea life, insects, plants and important elements from the woman's religion and daily life, the designs are believed to be filled with the spirits of the elements chosen. Each panel is unique, but mothers pass their designs down to daughters. A typical 16" x 16" panel takes months to make as 2-7 layers of bright solid cloth are cut and stitched. *Molas* are created from the top down starting with the large areas of the design on upper layers of cloth and working down to smaller areas at bottom layers of the cloth.

Peru

The beautifully patterned weaves of Peru are some of the finest textiles in the world. Wool is gathered from the native vicuña, llama, alpaca and wild guanaco (related to camel and llama.) The wool is colored using shells, insects and plants dyes. Peruvian women use hand spindles to spin the finest threads. Some of the hand weaving techniques used by the Peruvian artisans cannot be machine duplicated. Many of the textile patterns or motifs, such as the double-headed snake, are believed to represent families or ancient clans.

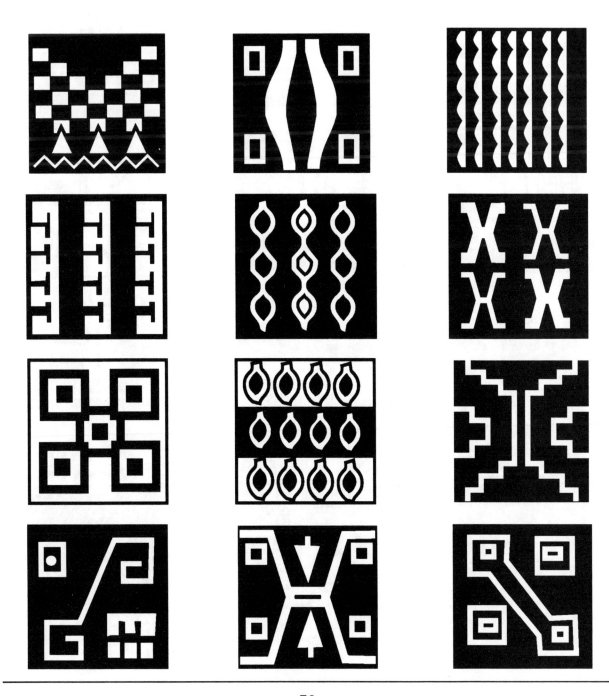

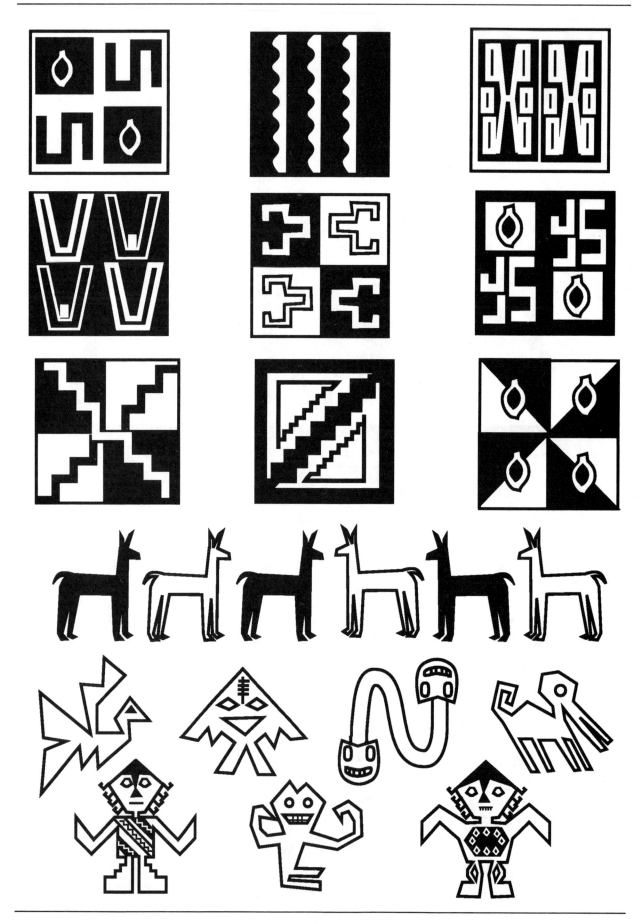

Arabic

Arabic artwork features geometric patterns that repeat and balance each other, linking or interfacing in a puzzle-like fashion, and moving the eye deeply into each design.

Turkish

Turkish artwork is a rich combination of bold, stylized patterns with stair-step designs and lovely nature motifs. Birds, flowers and vines cover every inch of space on artful ceramics, rugs, and tapestries. Even in an intricate border, you will see patterns repeat or intertwine.

  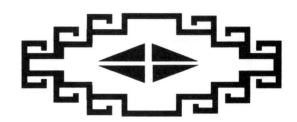

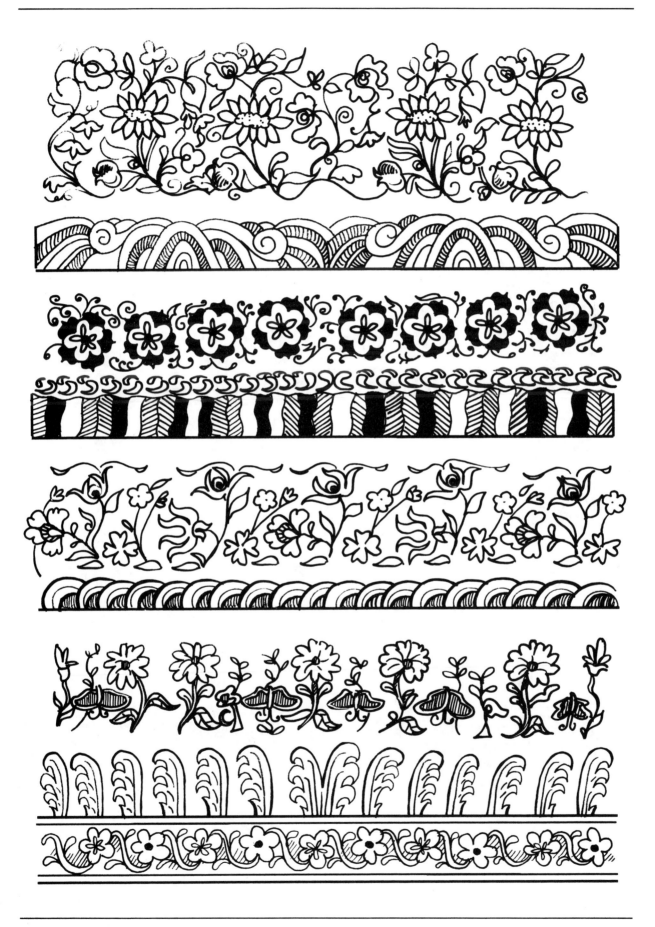

Persian

Persian art is very graceful and free-flowing. Plant motifs are used along with human figures and animals. Carefully planned symmetry and beautiful craftsmanship are typical of Persian paintings, mosaic tiles, enamelwork and carved fretwork. Artists use the finest materials available: Hand-made brushes, brilliant jewel-like pigments, and silver and gold accents.

Australia

Aborigines, the first Australians developed a style of bark painting that intrigues the eye and captures the imagination. The process involved stripping the bark off a eucalyptus tree, steaming it to remove the hard outer surface, and, finally, drying it underground. Paints were made from clay, carbon, ochre, water and plant juices to make the traditional colors of yellow, white and red. Brushes were made using twigs, leaves or feathers. From these simple materials, Aborigines created powerful images to celebrate their creation stories, culture and myths. Look closely to see the simple outlines filled with details so intricate that you feel you are looking at an X-ray. Some of the more complex paintings have the entire surface textured with fine lines and patterns.

South Pacific

An important textile art in Polynesia is called *tapa cloth*. Polynesians create these cloths by stripping inner layers of mulberry tree bark, soaking it in sea water and pounding it into ten-inch wide strips. Strips are then glued with *manioc* root juice to make sheets of cloth big enough for clothing, mats, room dividers and cloth for ceremonial decorations. Polynesians overlay, paint or stamp the cloth with patterns as diverse as the tropical paradise in which they live. The designs have an exuberant quality, with a high degree of skilled craftmanship. The sample patterns included for you to copy, cut and paste were re-created from many examples of original *tapa*. Polynesian artists also carved war canoes, clubs, houses and tools with exquisite geometric patterns and spiraling designs which they believed would identify them after their death.

Rarotonga Islands

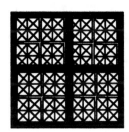

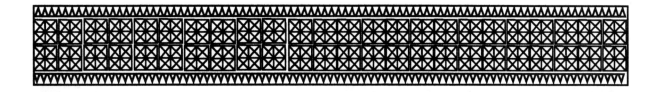

Tonga

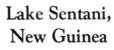
Lake Sentani,
New Guinea

Solomon Island

Sepic Area,
New Guinea

Colonial American

Colonial American art reflected the designs from countries of origin of the European peoples who came to America. Artists of this period used practical and simple designs, and bright and exuberant colors. Many of the designs used have a Christian significance. Colonial decorative art included painted ceramics, hand crafted and painted furniture, stitched quilts, and cross-stitched embroidery. A favorite decorative technique in colonial homes was stenciling. Using traditional designs and a small amount of paint, homes could be attractively embellished from ceiling to floors. Stencil artists often went from town to town offering their special skills to eager home owners.

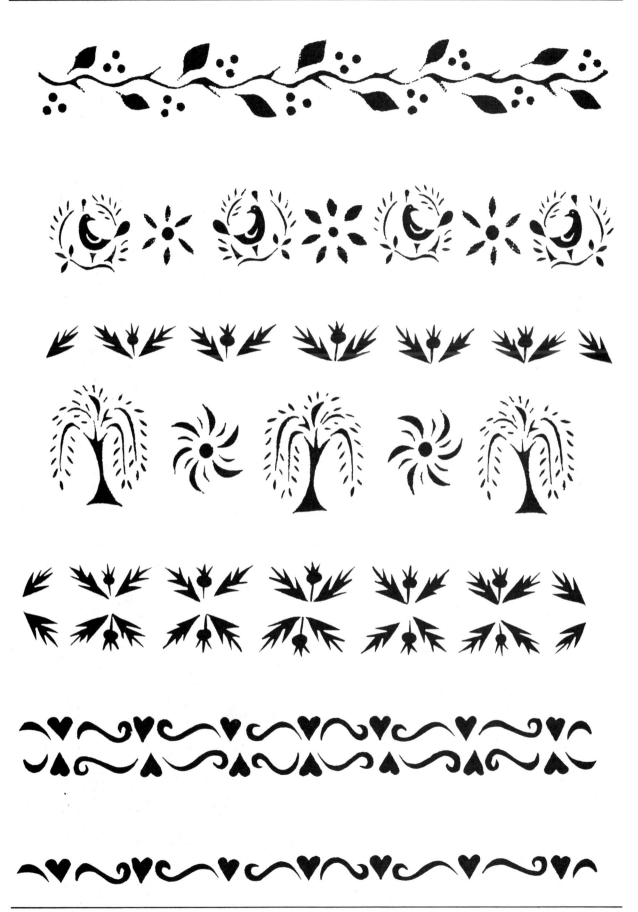

Symbols and their Meanings

tulip: trinity

grapevine: Christ

daisy: humilty

5 pointed star: birth of Christ

rooster: faithful

bald eagle: patriotism

oak/acorn: strength and endurance

stag: gentleness, pride

pineapple: hospitality

peacock: resurrection

sheep: Christ's flock

hearts: love

basket: giving

apple: evil

Hawaii

In Hawaii, artisan priests called *Kahunas* prayed and chanted as they created beautiful carvings from wood, ivory and shells. Hawaiians, like the Polynesians, stamped patterned cloth called *tapa cloth* (see patterns on pgs. 91- 94). A type of applique called *kapa-spana* developed when brightly colored cloth became available through trade. Women folded squares or circles of cloth and cut them to create a 4-8 sectioned symmetrical designs, then gathered in sewing circles to stitch the patterns onto light backgrounds. Designs were based on nature, stories, dreams or visions, and each family owned the patterns it created. Common shapes found in tapa designs included: crescent moons, flowers, plants, turtles, and octopuses. It was considered unlucky to cut human, bird, fish, or most animal shapes. Kapa-spana is still being crafted today.

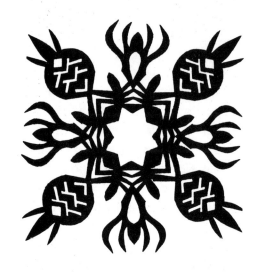

Native American

Native American artists of the Great Lakes used "naturalistic" art. Decorative flowers, leaves, and stems were stitched in concentric beaded rows (called spot stitching) on bags and clothing. Among the Chippewa, the designs were free flowing. Other tribes, such as the Winnebago in the southern Great Lakes, embroidered simpler symmetrical floral patterns.

Chippewa

Winnebago

Plains

Native American artists of the plains used rawhide rather than pottery, wood or bark for their art. Buffalo hides were prepared to make clothing, houses, bedding, folded envelopes for storage called *parfleches*, shields, belts and moccasins. Designs were painted or beaded in geometric patterns featuring stripes, diamonds, crosses, arrow, hour-glass shapes, thunderbird motifs, stars and hunting scenes.

Plains

Plains

Plains

Navaho

The Southwest has long been the most important weaving area. Along with the Hopi, Navaho Native Americans are the best weavers. Navaho women create beautiful geometric patterns on belt looms to make sashes, ties and garters for ceremonial costumes.

Hopi

Hopi is the largest of the Pueblo Native American groups. Common symbols used in Pueblo art are: birds, butterflies, bear claws, snakes, lizards, spiders, clouds, whirlwinds, rainbows and symbols for representing four directions. Some of these same elements are used to decorate beautiful coiled pottery with bold black, brown and white images. Weaving is done by the men in the tribe, and women create the basketry and pottery. Other images important in Hopi art are their *Kachinas*; over 300 designs that represent special Kachina spirits are believed to come to visit the Hopi.

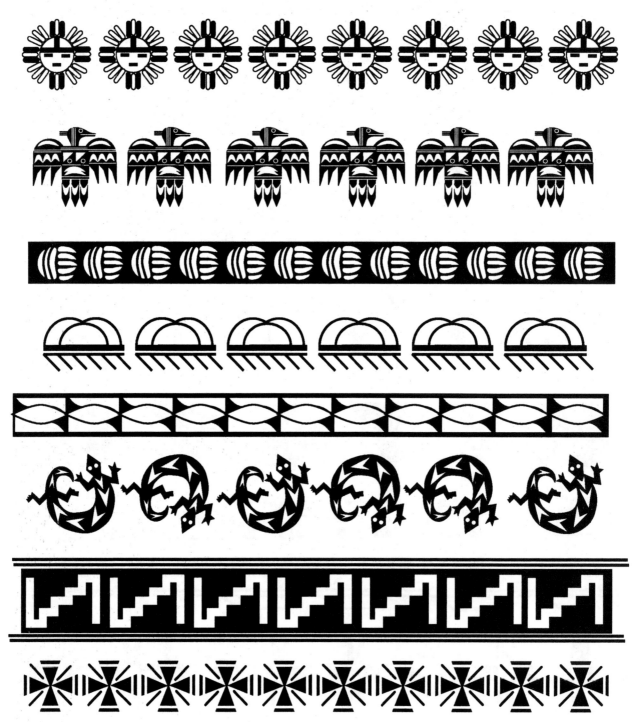

Hopi

Symbols and their Meanings

four directions:
north: yellow
south: red
east: white
west: blue-green

sun Kachina

clouds and rain

whirlwind

bear claw

water creature
(half turtle, half fish)

eagle

star

butterfly

snake

lizard

Northwest Coast

Northwest peoples believed in *totems*, meaning that each of their clans were closely related to a particular animal. Common totems included the raven, thunderbird, eagle, wolf, killer whale or bear. The chief purpose of their art was to represent their totem. It's size was stylized and adjusted to the shape of the object to which it was applied. Some designs looked flattened, bent or like an X-ray. Parts of the animals are drawn in squared ovals and solid, curved u-shaped sections.

Northwest Coast

Inuit

Inuit artists create sensitive, simple engraved animals, birds and descriptive scenes of daily life and travel. Inlaid appliqué work which include caribou and sealskin drawings are translated to cloth designs for traders. Stone sculptures of animals important to their life—the owl, polar bear, birds, reindeer and walrus—are also common. Inuit art gives a unique window into the daily life, dress, and beliefs of the native peoples of Canada.

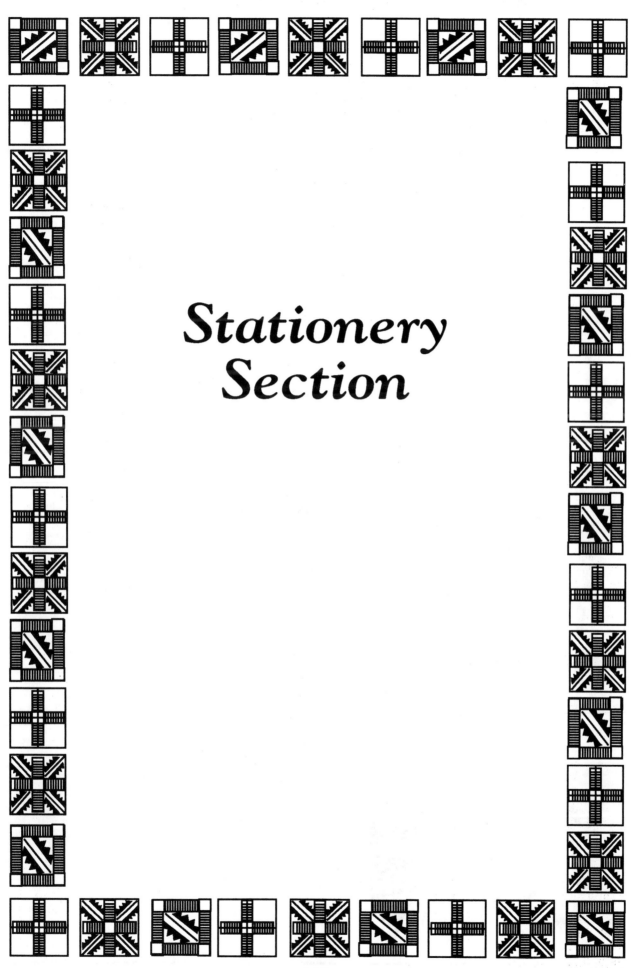

Stationery
Section

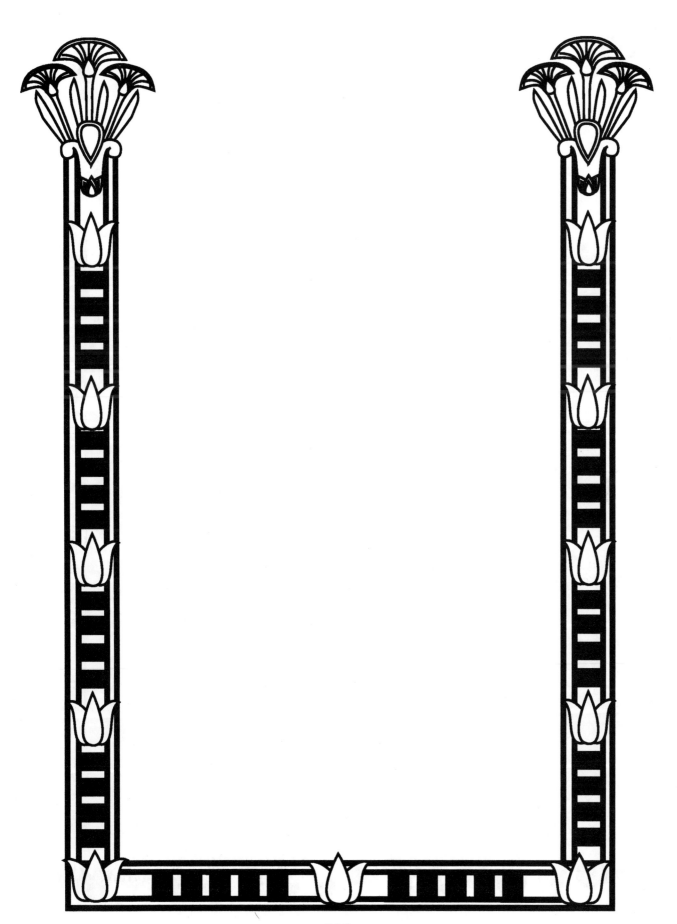